Babies

Nicola Baxter

W
FRANKLIN WATTS
LONDON•SYDNEY

You were a baby once.
Can you remember being a baby?
What is the first thing that you can
remember?

Try this later
Find a photograph of yourself as a baby.
Can your friends tell it is a picture of you?

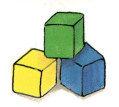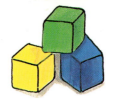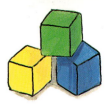

In fact, everyone was a baby once.
This picture shows a baby today
and the other one, a baby
nearly a hundred years ago.
Which one looks more comfortable?

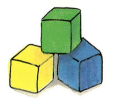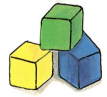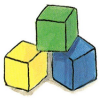

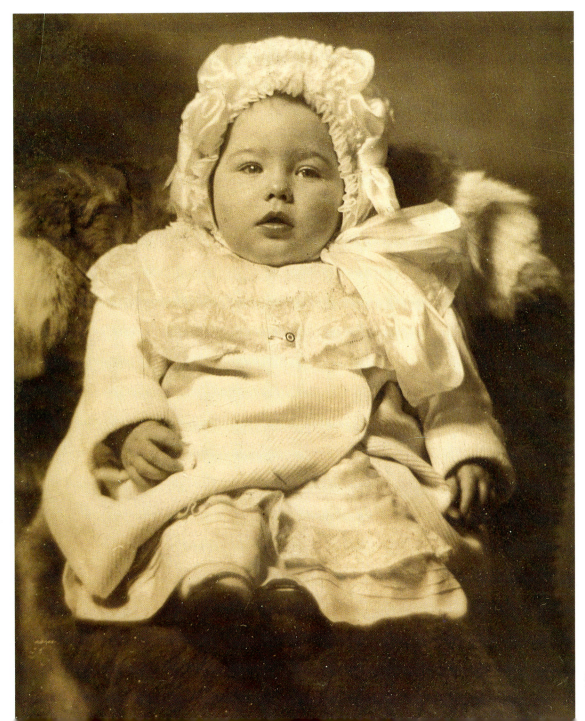

5

The day you were born was a special day.
On the same day each year you
celebrate your birthday with
your family and friends.

Ask someone to tell you the story of the day you were born.

When they are first born, babies can't talk or walk or even sit up by themselves. They have to be looked after carefully.

They sleep a lot of the time.
Sometimes they cry too.

New babies are fed by their mothers or
with special milk in bottles.
Later on they eat simple food.
But they can get very messy!

Babies have to be kept warm and safe.
They like to be cuddled!

Now try this

What have you learned to do since you were a baby?
Do you still like some of the things that babies like?

13

Babies soon learn to sit up and play.

Which of these toys do you think a baby would like?

When babies start to crawl - look out!
They want to find out about everything.

But they still have to be carried or
pushed when they go out.

Babies learn to walk by standing up...

and falling down...

and standing up...

18

and
falling
down...

until they can
do it!

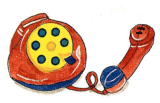

To start with babies make
all sorts of noises.
They learn to talk by listening
and copying.

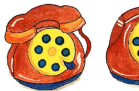   

Now try this
Pretend you haven't learned to talk yet.
Is it easy to make your friends understand you by making sounds and noises?

What happens to babies?
They grow up!
They learn to do all the things that you
can do - just like you did.

Index

birthday 6

crawling 16
crying 9

family 6
feeding 10
friends 3, 6

growing up 22

learning 13, 14, 16, 20, 22

looking after 8

milk 10
mothers 10

noises 20, 21

playing 14

sitting up 8, 14
sleeping 9

talking 8, 20, 21
toys 15

walking 8, 18-19

This edition 2003
Franklin Watts
96 Leonard Street
London EC2A 4XD

Franklin Watts Australia
45-51 Huntley Street
Alexandria NSW 2015

Copyright © Franklin Watts 1996
Editor: Sarah Ridley
Designer: Nina Kingsbury
Illustrator: Michael Evans

ISBN: 0 7496 5221 7

A CIP catalogue record for this book is available from the British Library.

Dewey Decimal Classification Number: 305.23

Acknowledgements:
The publishers would like to thank Tanya and Georgina Munn for their help with this book.

Additional photographs:
Bubbles 2, 7, 9, 10;
Collections 4, 14;
Mary Evans Picture Library 5;
Hutchison Library 12, 17;
Lupe Cunha Photos 20;
Peter Millard cover, 18, 19.

Printed in Malaysia